CONTENTS

YOUR CAT
FROM HEAD TO TAIL

Cats have lived with humans since the Ancient Egyptians welcomed them into their homes to keep snakes away and protect their grain stores from rats and mice. Cats are predators – they need to eat meat and their bodies have evolved to become awesome hunting machines.

Spine: Their flexible spine allows them to twist when they fall, and land on their feet.

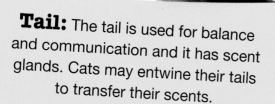

Tail: The tail is used for balance and communication and it has scent glands. Cats may entwine their tails to transfer their scents.

Back legs: Powerful back legs act like springs, allowing cats to jump up to nine times their height.

Claws: Claws are used for hunting, climbing and self-defence, but can be retracted to protect them and to allow cats to stalk their prey silently.

CATS

Published in Great Britain in 2018
by Wayland

Editor: Elizabeth Brent
Produced for Wayland by Dynamo
Written by Pat Jacobs

MIX
Paper from
responsible sources
FSC® C104740
FSC
www.fsc.org

ISBN: 9781526301406

10 9 8 7 6 5 4 3 2 1

Wayland, an imprint of
Hachette Children's Group
Part of Hodder and Stoughton
Carmelite House
50 Victoria Embankment
London EC4Y 0DZ

An Hachette UK Company
www.hachette.co.uk
www.hachettechildrens.co.uk

Printed and bound in China

Picture acknowledgements:

All images courtesy of iStock: p1 Tsekhmister; p2 Tomwang112, 5second, Joanna Zaleska; p3 GlobalP; p4 Eric Isselée, Elena Butinova; p5 Eric Isselée; p6 GlobalP, kipuxa, Axel Bueckert, cynoclub; p7 Lilun_Li, GlobalP, ewastudio, Kirill Vorobyev; p8 Pavel Hlystov, scigelova, Benjamin Simeneta, estevessabrina, Dixi_; p9 nevodka, Meinzahn, Eric Isselée, Erik Lam, chendongshan; p10 Ysbrand, Cosijn, parrus, Konstantin Aksenov, Mykola Velychko; p11 Axel Bueckert, eAlisa; p12 Yuriy Tuchkov, MW47, unclepodger; p13 Aly Tyler, Voren1, alexandco; p14 erjioLe, Aleksandr Ermolaev, GlobalP, detcreative; p15 Magone, aguirre_mar, gemenacom, Julián Rovagnati, anna1311, rvlsoft, Egor Shabanov, Nastco; p16 Dorottya_Mathe; p17 Okssi68, RalchevDesign, Goldfinch4ever, Ryerson Clark, alfonsmartin; p18 Bart_Kowski, Wavebreakmedia; p19 dny3d, Eric Isselée, MoosyElk, suemack, mashimara; p20 GlobalP; p21 Tony Campbell, oksun70, Maciej Maksymowicz; p22 cynoclub, adogslifephoto; p23 vvvita, Pavel Hlystov, gsermek; p24 Barna Tanko, Azaliya, Ikoimages; p25 cassinga, gurinaleksandr, absolutimages, Butsaya, mbolina; p26 GrishaL, Voren1, Leoba; p27 peplow, 2002lubava1981, GlobalP; p28 kmsh, Dixi_; p29 pwollinga; p32 MilanEXPO.Front cover : Dixi_; Back cover: fotostok_pdv
Every attempt has been made to clear copyright. Should there be any inadvertent omission, please apply to the publisher for rectification. The website addresses (URLs) included in this book were valid at the time of going to press. However, it is possible that contents or addresses may have changed since the publication of this book. No responsibility for any such changes can be accepted by either the author or the Publisher.

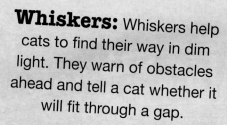

Ears: A cat's ear has around 30 muscles so it can swivel each one independently. Cats can detect high sounds that we can't hear and this helps them to pinpoint prey.

Eyes: Cats have a layer in their eyes that reflects light, so they can hunt in near-darkness. This is why cats' eyes glow at night.

Whiskers: Whiskers help cats to find their way in dim light. They warn of obstacles ahead and tell a cat whether it will fit through a gap.

Tongue: A cat's tongue has tiny backward-facing spikes to scrape meat from the bones of its prey and help with grooming.

Nose: A cat's sense of smell is far stronger than ours and it has an extra pair of scent organs, called Jacobson's organs, in the roof of its mouth.

CAT FACTS

- If a cat curls its lips and opens its mouth, it is using its Jacobson's organs to get information about an interesting scent.

- Pet cats usually live for about 15 years, but an American cat, called Creme Puff, died just after her 38th birthday!

Shoulders: Tiny collarbones attached to shoulder blades by muscle, not bone, mean cats can squeeze through spaces no larger than their head.

PEDIGREE CATS

There are more than 60 recognised breeds of cat, but most pet cats are a mix of breeds and come in all colours, shapes and sizes.

Siamese cats are affectionate and talkative – they are well-known for their loud yowls. They are intelligent, inquisitive and playful, so they do not like being left alone for long periods.

Bengal cats can leap to surprising heights, often performing somersaults in mid-air. They are noisy and energetic, and love to play with water.

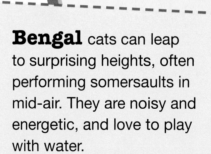

Sphynx cats look hairless, but most have fine, downy hairs. Their skin is marked as their fur would be. They are known for their friendly, dog-like behaviour and are intelligent and curious.

Abyssinians are very intelligent and inquisitive, with playful personalities. They enjoy going outdoors, are very active and enjoy the company of another cat.

Birmans have deep blue eyes, silky fur and white 'gloves' on each paw. They enjoy company, so don't like to be home alone. These quiet and curious cats will happily live with other pets.

Maine Coons are long-haired cats from America. They are excellent mousers and have tufted paws that allow them to walk on snow. These gentle giants get on well with other cats and dogs.

American Bobtail cats were bred from one American kitten with a very short tail. These fun-loving cats are great at escaping from places, and love to travel.

Devon Rex cats have a curly coat, large ears and an impish face. These mischievous cats love to climb. They are quick to learn tricks and enjoy playing fetch with other cats and dogs.

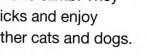

CHOOSING YOUR CAT

A cat is likely to be part of the family for many years, so before you fall in love with a cute kitten, it's a good idea to decide on the type of cat that will fit best into your household.

PEDIGREE MOGGY?

Pedigree kittens are more expensive than moggies (mixed breeds) and can have particular health problems, so buy one from a recommended breeder. Discovering what sort of cat your kitten will become is part of the fun of watching it grow.

KITTEN  ADULT CAT?

Kittens need lots of attention at first. Someone will need to be at home all day to keep an eye on them. Adult cats are more independent, but even older cats need time and attention to help them settle in.

LONG-HAIRED **OR** SHORT-HAIRED?

Long-haired cats shed hairs and need brushing every day. If you don't have time to brush them, a short-haired cat may be the best choice for you – and less grooming means more time for play!

MALE **OR** FEMALE?

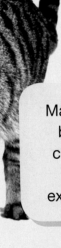

Male cats are slightly bigger than females, but if they are neutered there is little to choose between them. If you are buying a kitten, bear in mind that it is more expensive to neuter a female than a male.

INDOOR CAT **OR** OUTDOOR CAT?

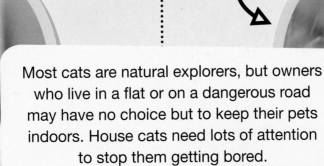

Most cats are natural explorers, but owners who live in a flat or on a dangerous road may have no choice but to keep their pets indoors. House cats need lots of attention to stop them getting bored.

COSY KITTY

Before you collect your new kitten or cat, you'll need some essential equipment to make your furry friend feel at home.

MEALTIME MUST-HAVES

Cats can be picky eaters, so buy a small selection of different foods to see which your cat prefers. Ceramic or stainless-steel bowls are best because some cats dislike the smell of plastic. Cats prefer wide, shallow bowls, so their whiskers don't brush against the sides.

PET CHECK ☑

Does your cat have:

- a litter tray in a quiet part of your home?
- food and water bowls?
- somewhere to scratch?

UNDERSTAND YOUR PET

I might feel nervous when I first move in, so please give me somewhere quiet to hide while I get to know my new home.

A reflective collar will help drivers to spot your cat if it goes out at night. It should snap or stretch if it gets caught so your cat can break free.

A strong and secure carrier with plenty of air holes is the safest way to bring your pet home and can be used for future trips to the vet.

You'll need a litter tray and a good supply of cat litter, along with a pooper-scooper to keep it clean. Place the tray away from your cat's eating and sleeping areas.

Cats scratch to mark their territory and keep their claws in tip-top condition so you will need a scratching post.

Even short-haired cats need weekly grooming, so a grooming brush is an essential piece of cat-care kit.

SETTLING IN

Bringing your cat home is very exciting, but it can be frightening for your new friend. Prepare one warm, quiet room with food and water, a litter tray and somewhere cosy to sleep, so your cat can feel safe while it gets used to its surroundings.

ON ARRIVAL

When you get home, take the cat carrier into the prepared room and open it, leaving your pet alone to explore its territory. Cats like to hide when they go somewhere new – a cardboard box makes a good hidey-hole.

MAKING FRIENDS

After a few hours, go into the room and sit quietly on the floor. You could take some toys and treats with you. Don't force your kitten to come to you or try to pick it up. If it is shy, it may take a few days before it feels confident enough to approach you.

STARTING TO EXPLORE

Your cat will let you know when it feels ready to explore the rest of your home by trying to follow you out of the room. Make sure all doors and windows leading outside are shut and keep the door to the cat's room open so it can escape there if it gets scared.

GOING OUTSIDE

Cats should be kept indoors for two weeks after their arrival to make sure they don't get lost. Let your cat out for a few minutes just before a meal, then stand at the door with some food to encourage it back inside.

MEETING OTHER PETS

Cats and dogs communicate using smell, so exchanging bedding between pets is a good way to get them used to one another before they meet. Keeping one animal in a crate or behind a pet barrier allows you to introduce them without risk of harm. Don't leave two pets alone together until you are certain they have become friends.

CATERING FOR KITTY

Cats are carnivores and need to eat meat. Unlike dogs, they cannot survive on a vegetarian diet. Cats like to eat little and often, so only feed them small amounts at a time and don't leave food lying around as it will attract flies.

FEEDING KITTENS

Because kittens grow so fast, they need more food than adult cats. They can start eating small amounts of kitten food at about four weeks old and should be fully weaned at the age of eight weeks.

FEEDING CATS

The easiest way to make sure your cat is getting all the nutrients it needs is to buy a good-quality cat food. Many cats prefer wet food, but they don't like it cold, so keep unopened sachets or tins at room temperature.

Dried food is useful if you have to leave it out during the day.

UNDERSTAND YOUR PET

Please don't feed me human foods, such as chocolate, onions and garlic, because they could make me ill.

WEIGHT WATCHING

As pet cats don't have to chase their prey and have a regular supply of food, they can easily become overweight. A fat cat can suffer from health problems, so don't give yours too many treats.

DRINKING

Although cats don't drink much, fresh water should be available at all times, especially if your pet is eating dried food.

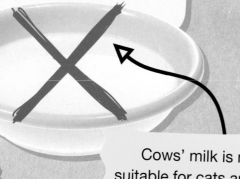

Cows' milk is not suitable for cats and can cause stomach upsets.

WEIGHT CHECK ✓

- You should be able to feel your cat's bones beneath a thin layer of fat.
- Your cat should have a narrower waist behind the ribs when you look at it from above and from the side.

DAY-TO-DAY CARE

Check your pet for any sign of illness or injury every day. If your cat seems to be in pain or has stopped eating, it's time to visit the vet. It's much better to deal with any problems quickly so your furry friend doesn't suffer unnecessarily.

GROOMING

Brush your cat regularly – especially if it has long hair. This gets rid of loose hairs, which cats may swallow, and it's a good opportunity to check your pet for injuries. If cats swallow a lot of fur, hairballs form in their stomach and the cat will bring them up.

UNDERSTAND YOUR PET

I don't make a fuss if I feel ill, so it's important for my owner to notice any changes in my behaviour.

FLEAS

Cat fleas are very common. They are tiny, but you might spot them when you are grooming your cat. There are many products to keep your pet flea-free, but make sure you choose the right one as some dog-flea treatments contain chemicals that are harmful to cats.

WORMING

Cats can pick up roundworms or tapeworms from other animals, from eating infected prey or from fleas. They often don't show any sign of a worm infestation unless it is serious so it's best to give your cat a worming tablet regularly.

TOOTH CARE

Taking care of your cat's teeth is a top priority. Cat toothpaste comes in fish or meat flavours, so start by letting your cat taste a little, then just touch its teeth with a cat toothbrush. As your pet gets used to the idea, start brushing its teeth gently.

HEALTH AND SAFETY

You can help to keep your cat safe by understanding what could harm it. Store medicines and household products out of reach, keep upstairs windows closed and arrange yearly check-ups with your vet to make sure your pet stays fit and well.

VACCINATIONS

All kittens should be vaccinated against common cat diseases and will need regular booster vaccines as they grow. When you get a cat, check which vaccinations it has had and when the next ones are due.

NEUTERING

Kittens should be neutered when they are four months old. This will stop them wandering off and protects them against some diseases. An unneutered female cat could give birth to up to 200 kittens in her lifetime and an unneutered male is more likely to get into fights and spray urine to mark his territory.

UNDERSTAND YOUR PET

I don't like going to the vet, but you can make it less scary for me by putting some of my bedding in the carrier so it smells like home.

MICROCHIPPING

A microchip is the size of a grain of rice and is inserted under the cat's skin by a vet. If a lost cat is found, the microchip can be read and matched to the owner's contact details so they can be reunited.

POISONS

If you think your cat has been poisoned, take it to the vet at once. Cats may eat poisoned prey, such as mice, and some plants are dangerous for cats, especially those in the lily family. Cats may not swallow harmful substances on purpose, but could lick them off their fur.

TRAFFIC ACCIDENTS

If you live near a busy road, you can reduce the risk of your cat being run over by keeping it in at night. Feed your cat at dusk, to encourage it to come in before it gets dark.

PET CHECK

Has your cat been:

- neutered?
- vaccinated?
- microchipped?

CAT BEHAVIOUR

In the wild, cats hunt alone and each needs a territory large enough to provide enough to eat. Most male cats live on their own, but females and kittens may live in groups if there's plenty of food to go round. Pet cats are usually happy living alone, but some enjoy the company of other cats, especially if they have grown up together.

HIGH SPOTS

Cats like to observe their surroundings from a high place, so they can search for prey and watch out for danger. Many cats like to sit on a raised perch at home too, and if you have more than one cat, the leader will usually have the highest spot.

TAKING A CATNAP

Cats sleep for about two thirds of their lives, which means they are asleep for about 16 hours a day. They are most likely to be wide awake at dawn and dusk, which is when their prey is most active.

UNDERSTAND YOUR PET

I am most active in the early mornings and in the evening. That's the best time to play with me.

SCRATCHING

This is part of a cat's natural behaviour. Cats have scent glands between their toes and it's one of the ways they mark their territory. Encourage your pet to use a scratching post by rubbing it with catnip and sprinkling some treats around the base.

HUNTING

Your cat is programmed to hunt prey, even when it has plenty of food. You can help to satisfy this instinct by playing 'cat and mouse' games with your pet, but don't be surprised if you still get a present of a dead mouse or bird!

COMMUNICATION

Understanding how cats talk to each other will help you to work out what your cat is trying to tell you. Cats don't just communicate using sound – body language and scent are equally important to them.

BODY TALK

A cat's tail and ears are good clues to its mood. If its tail is straight up in the air and its ears are pricked up, the cat is feeling friendly, but if its tail is swishing from side to side and its ears are back, watch out – this is a warning that the cat is annoyed and may attack.

EYE CONTACT

When two cats meet they may challenge one another by staring, so your cat might not enjoy being stared at. A relaxed cat will blink or wink, and when your cat squints at you, that's the feline equivalent of a smile.

UNDERSTAND YOUR PET

I might roll over on my back if I feel relaxed or want to play-fight, but don't try to touch my tummy or I will probably scratch you.

SUPER SNIFFERS

Cats have a great sense of smell. They use the scent glands on their faces, tails and between their toes to communicate. When a cat rubs its face on something or someone, it's marking its home turf and the members of its family group.

CAT CHAT

Cats chirp and miaow as a greeting or to tell you it's time to get up, give them food, or whatever else they might want. When they get angry, they will hiss, snarl and growl. Cats purr when they are happy and relaxed, but sick or injured cats may purr too, to comfort themselves.

TRAINING

The best way to train your cat is to use a clicker and treats. Punishing your cat for bad behaviour won't work, and could frighten it. The first step is to get your cat to understand the connection between the clicker and a treat, by giving your cat a tasty reward after each click.

CLICKER

CHECKING IN

Getting your cat to come when called is useful if your pet goes outside, and could save it from danger. Practise in one room by calling the cat's name and pressing the clicker. Give your pet a treat as soon as it comes to you. When your cat has got the idea, try calling from a different room or from outside.

UNDERSTAND YOUR PET

It's important to give me my treat every time I do what you ask me to, otherwise I may not do it next time.

TOILET TRAINING

Take your kitten to its litter tray when it wakes up and after every meal, then give it a reward for using the tray. Keep the tray in the same place and replace the litter regularly. Don't use disinfectant or chemicals to clean it as they may harm your cat.

MAKE A CAT RATTLE

Cats are sensitive to noise so if your pet is scratching the furniture or jumping on the dining table, a sharp noise will send a message that this is not acceptable. Make a noisy cat rattle to discourage unwanted behaviour by putting some pebbles in a tin with a lid.

HIGH FIVES

Hold up your hand with a treat wedged between the fingers. When your pet puts its paw up to get the treat, press the clicker and give it the reward. After you have practised this, try the trick without the treat.

FUN AND GAMES

Cats love to play. It keeps them fit and alert and it's fun for their owners, too. Cats like toys that move so they can practise their hunting skills. There's no need to spend a lot of money though – you can easily make your own.

Cats are very inquisitive and enjoy climbing and hiding, so a few cardboard boxes with entry and exit holes will keep them entertained for hours.

Throw a lightweight ball up the stairs so your cat can run after it as it rolls down.

Make a fishing-pole toy by tying feathers or tissue paper to some string or a stick and wave it close to your cat.

CATNIP CRAZY

Catnip is a herb that many adult cats go mad for. They love to sniff it, lick it, rub against it and roll in it. You can try growing some in a pot at home, or buy a cheap toy filled with dried catnip to see how your pet reacts.

Cats love chasing games. Try stuffing an old sock inside another and tying it to string. Drag it along in front of your cat using slow pulls and sharp jerks.

Blow some bubbles for your cat to chase.

TOP TIPS!

- Play for a short time every day
- Let your cat catch the toy at the end of each game
- Rotate toys so your cat doesn't get bored
- Tidy away toys after play to avoid accidents

CAT QUIZ

By now you should know lots of things about cats.

Test your knowledge by answering these questions:

1 **How long does the average cat live?**

   a. 5 years

   b. 15 years

   c. 30 years

2 **What are Jacobson's organs used for?**

   a. Seeing at night

   b. Scent marking

   c. Smelling

3 **What is unusual about a Sphynx cat?**

   a. It is almost hairless

   b. It has a curly coat

   c. It has a short tail

4 **How many hours does a cat sleep each day?**

   a. 8

   b. 16

   c. 20

5 **Can a cat be a vegetarian?**

   a. Yes

   b. Partly

   c. No

6 Which plant makes some cats go crazy?

a. Catnip
b. Parsley
c. Mint

10 Which of these foods is harmful to cats?

a. Chocolate
b. Onions
c. Both of these

7 How is a cat feeling if its tail is swishing and its ears are back?

a. Happy
b. Relaxed
c. Angry

8 How many kittens will an average cat have during her life if she is not neutered?

a. 50
b. 200
c. 600

9 How often should you groom a short-haired cat?

a. Every day
b. Every week
c. Every month

QUIZ ANSWERS

1 How long does the average cat live?

b. 15 years

2 What are Jacobson's organs used for?

c. Smelling

3 What is unusual about a Sphynx cat?

a. It is almost hairless

4 How many hours does a cat sleep each day?

b. 16

5 Can a cat be a vegetarian?

c. No

6 Which plant makes some cats go crazy?

a. Catnip

7 How is a cat feeling if its tail is swishing and its ears are back?

c. Angry

8 How many kittens will an average cat have during her life if she is not neutered?

b. 200

9 How often should you groom a short-haired cat?

b. Every week

10 Which of these foods is harmful to cats?

c. Both of these

GLOSSARY

breed – Named cat breeds have special features, such as a particular body shape or fur pattern, and all members of a breed will look more or less the same.

carnivore – An animal that eats mainly meat.

feline – Another word for cat or cat-like.

gland – An organ that makes fluids and chemicals, such as saliva, sweat and tears. Most animals have scent glands that produce a personal smell, which they use to mark their territory.

hairball – When a cat grooms itself, it swallows hair, which forms a ball in its stomach. Cats get rid of these balls by being sick.

infestation – A number of insects, worms or other creatures large enough to cause damage.

instinct – Natural behaviour that is automatic, not learned, such as a cat's ability to hunt.

Jacobson's organs – If a cat wants information about a smell, it uses its tongue to flick the scent up to these tube-like organs in the roof of its mouth. They recognise chemicals in smells such as urine as well as chemical signals given by other cats.

microchip – A microchip is a tiny electronic device, the size of a grain of rice. It has a number that is stored on a computer with a record of the owner's name and address. A scanner will show the number so a lost cat's owner can be found.

mixed-breed – A mixed-breed cat has parents from at least two different breeds.

neutering – An operation that stops cats having kittens.

nutrients – Food contains different nutrients, including protein, vitamins and minerals. All animals need these to survive and grow.

pedigree – An animal that has two pure-bred parents of the same breed.

predator – An animal that hunts and eats other creatures.

prey – An animal that is hunted by others.

programmed – Acting in a way that is part of natural behaviour.

retract – To pull in (e.g. claws).

roundworms – White or light brown worms that live in cats' intestines. They can be passed to humans, so avoid touching used cat litter and always wash your hands after cleaning the litter tray.

tapeworms – Worms that look like ribbons. They are passed to cats when they swallow a flea or eat the liver of a mouse or rat that contains the worms' eggs.

vaccination – Injections that protect cats from serious diseases, such as feline enteritis and cat flu. They should have their first injections as kittens, with booster (follow-up) injections every few years.

vegetarian – Food that does not include meat or fish. Cats cannot survive on this kind of diet – they need to eat meat, with fish as a treat now and again.

weaning – Introducing a kitten to solid food. Kittens should have small amounts of kitten food, as well as their mother's milk, from the age of four weeks and be eating just solid food by about eight weeks old.

INDEX